The Nutella Cookbook: Heavenly Nutella Recipes That Will Leave You Wanting More

Disclaimer and Terms of Use: Effort has been made to ensure that the information in this book is accurate and complete, however, the author and the publisher do not warrant the accuracy of the information, text and graphics contained within the book due to the rapidly changing nature of science, research, known and unknown facts and internet. The Author and the publisher do not hold any responsibility for errors, omissions or contrary interpretation of the subject matter herein. This book is presented solely for motivational and informational purposes only.

Table of Contents

Coffee Pie Nutella

Ingredients:
- Graham Cracker crust
- 12 oz. package chocolate chips
- 2 T butter
- 1 ¼ C heavy cream
- 2 T ground coffee beans
- 2 egg whites ½ C sugar

Directions:

I. Use prepared premade graham cracker pie crust
II. Place chocolate and butter in a bowl
III. Boil coffee, cream, and water in small saucepan and remove from heat and let sit for about 5 minutes
IV. For your meringue use mixer to beat egg whites and add sugar until frothy
V. Spook meringue over coffee granules and swirl
VI. Add mixture to pie crust and chill

Ingredients:
- 2 ½ C flour
- 3 ½ oz. sugar
- ½ tsp salt
- 2 eggs
- 1 ¾ C whole milk
- 1 ½ oz. yeast
- 6 C grape seed oil
- 1 jar Nutella

Directions:

I. Mix the first three ingredients, and stir eggs and half of your milk whisking until well mixed
II. Warm rest of milk with the yeast and stir until yeast dissolves.
III. Cover and let set for about 5-6 hours
IV. Heat up skillet, and add oil, and fry the brittle for about 5 minutes each
V. Let them set and drain grease,
VI. Using pastry bag fill each one with Nutella and let sit

Ingredients:

- 300 g almond meal
- 300icing sugar
- 60 cocoa
- Egg whites
- 30 ml coffee
- 1 tsp vanilla extract
- Caster sugar
- 75ml water
- Egg whites
- Chopped milk chocolate
- Double cream
- Butter
- Nutella

Directions:

I. Line baking sheet with parchment paper, sift your meal, sugar and cocoa, mixing paper
II. Add egg whites, coffee and vanilla into your drifted ingredients, and set aside DO NOT MIX
III. Make your meringue and mix, into stiff meringue
IV. Boil sugar and water, watch with a candy thermometer add egg whites
V. Fold meringue into almond meal mix, making three batches
VI. Create macaroons

Pound cake

Ingredients:

- 1 12 C flour
- 4 eggs
- 2 tsp pure vanilla extract
- ¾ tsp baking powder
- ¼ tsp salt
- 2 sticks butter
- 1 ¼ C sugar
- 1 jar Nutella

Directions:

I.   Preheat your oven to 350 degrees
II. In bowl whisk dry ingredients, in separate bowl mix wet ingredients
III. Combine both bowls
IV. Add one thin layer to bottom of pan of cake mix followed by layer of Nutella, Repeat layers until both mixes are gone
V.   Bake for about 1 hour and 15 minutes
VI. Turn upside down and let cool for at least 2 hours

Caramel Ice cream sandwiches

Ingredients:
- 1 C hazelnut
- 1 C powdered sugar
- 2 T flour
- 4 large egg whites
- Salt
- ¼ sugar
- 4 oz. chocolate chips
- C Nutella 6 Sugar cones
- 1 pint ice-cream

Directions:

I. Preheat your oven to 350 degrees, line sheet with parchment paper, roast nuts for 12 minutes or so

II. Add nuts, powdered sugar and flour to food processor, until nuts are ground

III. In bowl beat egg whites, salt. You want them to be stiff, making a peak Fold in nuts

IV. Spread everything on the parchment paper and bake for 20 minutes or so

V. Let sit for one hour

VI. Melt chocolate chips in microwave and stir in Nutella with CRUSHED waffle cones

VII. Spread with Nutella filling and cut into squares, and freeze.

VIII. Serve with Ice-cream

Cappuccino

Ingredients:
- 2 C milk
- ½ C Nutella
- ½ T espresso powder

Directions:

I.   Add milk into saucepan, and bring to a steady simmer, then pour into blender, add remaining two ingredients, and run blender on medium. You want everything well blended. Spoon into mugs and serve.

Devil's food cake

Ingredients:
- 2 1/3 C flour
- Cooking spray
- 1 C cocoa powder
- 1 ½ tsp baking soda
- 1 tsp salt
- ¼ tsp baking powder
- 2 tsp espresso powder
- 1 C HOT coffee
- 1 C buttermilk
- 2 ½ C sugar
- 2 sticks butter
- 4 eggs
- 1 ½ tsp vanilla extract
- 1 bag chocolate chips (melted and cooled)
- ¼ C hazelnuts
- 3 C rice cereal
- 12 C Nutella
- 8 oz. milk
- 8 oz. chocolate chips
- 1 ½ T corn syrup
- 1 ½ C heavy cream
- 2 sticks butter

Directions:

I. Preheat oven to 350 degrees and spray baking pans

II. Sift your dry ingredients and set aside

III. Dissolve espresso into the hot coffee and add the buttermilk

IV. In mixer beat your sugar, butter until light and fluffy, add eggs, slowly, one at a time, and beat in vanilla. Beat until light and fluffy

V. Beat in flour and remaining ingredients and add coffee mixture divide batter between two cake pans

VI.   Bake for 25-30 minutes and let cool
VII.   For the hazelnut you line set with parchment paper and toast nuts, and chop add chocolate and butter in bowl, stirring.
VIII.   Stir in hazelnuts and Nutella and freeze for about 30 minutes
IX.   Make frosting last and frost your cake top with hazelnut crunch

Nut buns

Ingredients:
- 1 pkg. dry yeast
- ¼ C sugar
- ½ C milk
- 9T butter
- 1 t salt
- 1 tsp vanilla
- 3 eggs
- 4 C flour
- ¾ C brown sugar
- 2/3 C chopped pecans
- 1 ½ C Nutella
- 1 tsp ground cinnamon

Directions:

I. Add yeast, 1 T sugar, and ½ C water in bowl for about 10 minutes. Bring milk to aimer in pan and set aside. Stir in mixture sugar butter and salt, add remaining ingredients slowly
II. Stir constantly
III. Pour into greased bowl and let set for just under 2 hours
IV. Preheat oven to 375 and bake for 30 minutes.
V. Add pecans and sugar making frosting. Add once cooled

Hot chocolate liqueur

Ingredients:
- 3 T Nutella
- 1 1/3 C milk

Directions:

I. Mix tow ingredients together over medium heat in skillet until well blended
II. Whisk until frothy and serve

Hot Chocolate

Ingredients:
- Cocoa Powder
- Nutella
- Milk

Directions:

I. Mix everything in slow cooker for 2 hours

Nutella Oreo Pie

Ingredients:
- 1 pkg. Oreos
- 1/3 C butter

Pie Filling

- 1 C Nutella
- 1 pkg. Cream cheese
- Cool whip (thawed)
- ½ C Chopped Nutellas

Directions:

I.   Add crust ingredients to food processor and scoop into pie crust pressing into bottom of pie crust
II. For filling add everything together and refrigerate for a few hour, then spoon into crust and let cool again for 5-15 minutes

Grilled Nutella Sandwiches

Ingredients:
- Bread
- 2 T Nutella
- Mini marshmallows
- 2 T butter

Directions:

I.   Spread Nutella over bread and add marshmallows on top
II.   Grill over skillet until marshmallows melt

Pumpkin Spice Nutella

Ingredients:
- 2 1/ C milk
- 1/3 C hot cocoa mix
- ¼ C pumpkin
- 1 ½ tsp pumpkin pie spice
- 1 T Nutella

Directions:

I.   Heat over medium heat whisking well.
II.   Once warm enough to your preference, serve

Ingredients:
- 8 C Apple cider
- ¼ C brown sugar
- 1 T Nutella
- 1 tsp allspice
- 1 tsp cloves

Directions:

I.   Heat everything in sauce pan or slow cooker until everything is warm, and dissolved. Serve in mugs

Chocolate Bisque

Ingredients:
- Heavy cream
- Whole milk
- Sugar
- 1 vanilla bean
- 1 T Nutella
- 2 stick cinnamon
- Zest of orange
- 3 slices ginger
- Cocoa powder
- 3 T coffee ground
- 6 egg yolks
- Chocolate chips

Directions:

I.   Melt everything in saucepan until completely melted or dissolved

Ingredients:

- 6 C 2 5 milk
- 2 C half and half
- 12 oz. white chocolate chips
- 1 T Nutella
- Whipped cream for Garnish topping

Directions:

I.   Add everything to saucepan and heat over medium heat, stirring frequently.

II.   Wait until everything is melted or dissolved and serve

Almond Nutella Chocolate

Ingredients:
- ¾ C heavy cream
- ½ C marshmallow cream
- 2 T almond liquor
- ¼ tsp vanilla extract

Chocolate filling

- 1 can coconut milk
- 2 T Nutella
- 3 T brown sugar
- ½ C chocolate chips

Directions:

I.   Heat first set of ingredients on a slow simmer, melt chocolate ingredients until well dissolved and or melted.
II. Pour chocolate into boiling mixture and turn down heat, stir frequently.
III. Serve

Ingredients:

- I C almond milk
- ½ C butterscotch chips
- 1 T Nutella
- 1-2 tsp Rum

Directions:

I.   Mix everything over low to medium heat and stir frequently

Peanut Butter Latte

Ingredients:

- ¾ C almond milk
- 2 T cocoa powder
- 1 T Nutella
- 1 tsp agave
- 1 shot espresso

Directions:

I.   Heat everything over low to medium heat, and serve

Ingredients:
- ¾ C brown sugar
- ½ C butter
- 1 tsp vanilla extract
- ½ tsp cinnamon
- 1 T Nutella
- ¼ tsp allspice
- 3 C Rum

Directions:

I. Combine and crush all of the herbs and spices, and add to liquids, boiling, dissolving the Nutella and spices, bring to a simmer
II. Serve (this is for adults only)

Cholate Latte

Ingredients:
- 2 ¼ C almond milk
- 1 C espresso
- 1-2 T Nutella

Directions:

I.   Using an espresso machine or Keurig create your latte with the above mentioned ingredients.

Spicy Chocolate Cranberry Drink

Ingredients:
- 4 Qtrs. Water
- 5 C frozen cranberries
- 2 ½ C sugar
- ½ C red hot candies
- 3 T Nutella

Directions:

I. Mix everything together in HOT water, from a boil bring down to a simmer
II. Serve

CPSIA information can be obtained
at www.ICGtesting.com
Printed in the USA
LVOW04s0051221116

513925LV00065B/1671/P